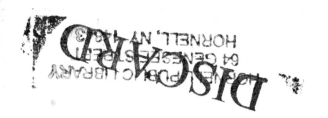

A TEEN GUIDE *to* BREAKFAST *on the Go*

by Dana Meachen Rau

CONTENT ADVISER: Joan Bushman, MPH, RD,
Dietician and Wellness Specialist

READING ADVISER: Alexa L. Sandmann, EdD, Professor of Literacy,
College of Education, Health, and Human Services,
Kent State University

COMPASS POINT BOOKS
a capstone imprint

Compass Point Books
151 Good Counsel Drive
P.O. Box 669
Mankato, MN 56002-0669

Editor: Jennifer Fretland VanVoorst
Designers: Veronica Correia and Heidi Thompson
Media Researcher: Wanda Winch
Food Stylist: Sarah Schuette
Library Consultant: Kathleen Baxter
Production Specialist: Sarah Bennett

Image Credits

ArtParts Stock Illustrations, illustrations of food and cookware used throughout book; Capstone Studio: Karon Dubke, cover (all top), 15, 17, 19, 21, 23, 27, 29, 31, 35, 37, 39, 41, 43, 44–45, 47, 49, 51, 53; Dana Meachen Rau, 64 (middle); Getty Images Inc.: Blend Images, 60; iStockphoto: Anthony Boulton, cover (bottom right), 1, 4–5, ariwasabi, 24 (middle), Daniel Bendjy, cover (bottom middle left), 33, digitalskillet, 63 (top), Don Bayley, 6–7, Kati Molin, 57, knape, 8, 12-13, Ned White, 24 (bottom right), Pascal Genest, 24 (back); Shutterstock: Andrjuss, 13 (bottom), Anna Subbotina, back cover, 11 (bottom), blueking, cover (bottom left), 32 (left), D. Copy, 6 (top left) Elena Schweitzer, 54 (top), Elke Dennis, 59 (left), fantasista, 9, Ian O'Hanlon, 100% stamp design, Jaren Jai Wicklund, 62 (left), lev dolgachov, cover (bottom middle right), Maksim Shmeljov, 58–59 (bottom), 62–63 (bottom), 64 (bottom), Monkey Business Images, 32 (right), Thaiview, cover background, 10–11 (background), Valentyn Volkov, 7 (bottom right), Yuri Arcurs, 59 (right), ZanyZeus, 25.

Library of Congress Cataloging-in-Publication Data
Rau, Dana Meachen, 1971–
  A Teen guide to breakfast on the go / by Dana Meachen Rau.
    p. cm. — (Teen cookbooks)
  Includes index.
    ISBN 978-0-7565-4407-2 (library binding)
1. Breakfasts—Juvenile literature. 2. Cookbooks. I. Title. II. Title:
Breakfast on the go.
  TX733.R38 2011
  642—dc22   2010038580

Visit Compass Point Books on the Internet at *www.capstonepub.com*

Printed in the United States of America in North Mankato, Minnesota.

092010

005933CGS11

TABLE OF CONTENTS

Energy to Face Your Day 4

Hitting the Store 6

How to Avoid 8

How to Use This Book 10

YOU CAN'T BEAT EGGS! 12

Skyscraper Sandwich 14

Scrambled Salsa Burrito 16

Quick Quiches... 18

Hidden Sunshine French Toast.. 20

Party Cakes... 22

BREAKFAST BOWLS 24

Oatmeal Chocolate Chip Cookie in a Bowl 26

Power Cereal... 28

Banana Cream Pie in a Bowl 30

ON THE GO 32

Smooth Moves... 34

Go Nuts Nuggets 36

Bad Breath Bagels 38

Hold the Phone ... and a Scone! 40

PB&J Muffins 42

ON THE SIDE 44

Mohawk Mango Heads 46

Apes and Grapes Salad 48

Orange Cream Juice 50

Red-Hot Cocoa 52

Chew on This... 54

Tools Glossary 56

Technique Glossary 58

Additional Resources 61

Index.. 62

ENERGY TO FACE YOUR DAY

Your math teacher announces that instead of algebra and geometry, you'll be learning how to shoot spitballs at a target on the wall. And did he really just pull out a banjo? Can it be true? Is math suddenly becoming fun?

You're thinking school isn't so bad after all, when suddenly ...

BEEP! BEEP! BEEP! The alarm goes off. You press the snooze button.

Now the teacher is moving out the desks and replacing them with lounge chairs. He's serving ice-cold lemonade ...

BEEP! BEEP! BEEP! There goes that alarm again. It was all a dream.

How many times can you hit the snooze button and still have time to eat breakfast? You don't want to set that alarm any earlier than you have to. But breakfast doesn't have to take much time. If you have a few spare minutes in the morning, you can make yourself a quick, nutritious meal to start the day.

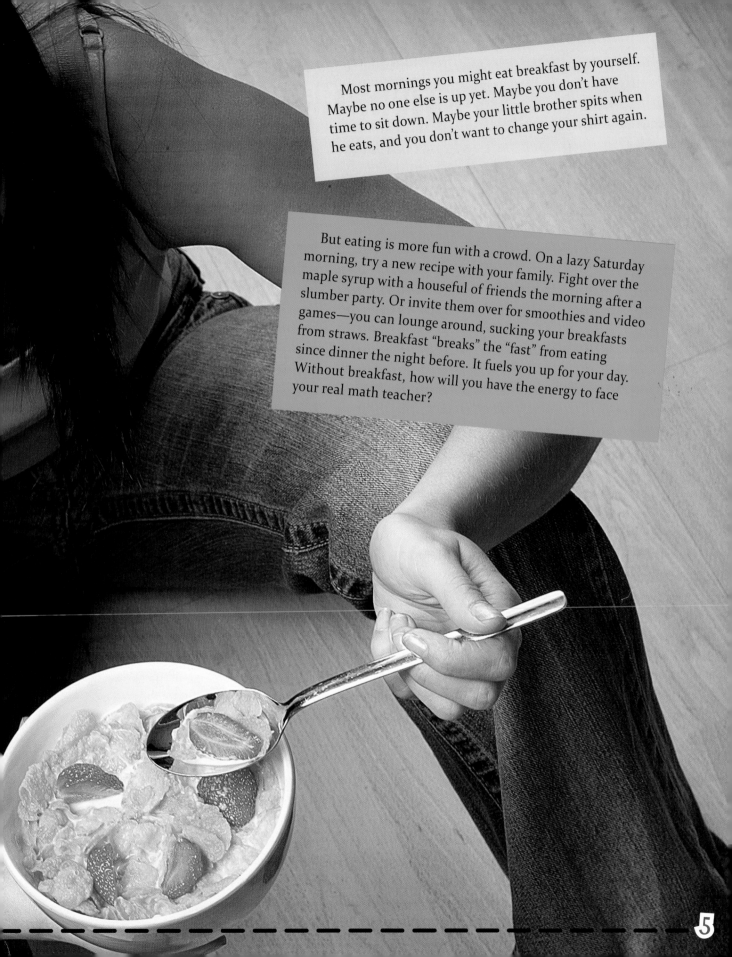

Most mornings you might eat breakfast by yourself. Maybe no one else is up yet. Maybe you don't have time to sit down. Maybe your little brother spits when he eats, and you don't want to change your shirt again.

But eating is more fun with a crowd. On a lazy Saturday morning, try a new recipe with your family. Fight over the maple syrup with a houseful of friends the morning after a slumber party. Or invite them over for smoothies and video games—you can lounge around, sucking your breakfasts from straws. Breakfast "breaks" the "fast" from eating since dinner the night before. It fuels you up for your day. Without breakfast, how will you have the energy to face your real math teacher?

A great day starts with a great breakfast. And a great breakfast starts with great ingredients.

When you're shopping for groceries, the most important tip is to buy fresh.

Produce

Piles of pears! Mounds of mangoes! How do you know if something is fresh? If a fruit or vegetable has lots of brown or mushy spots, don't buy it. It's probably been sitting there awhile. Most fruits are firm when unripe and soften when ripe. On the other hand, most vegetables are best when they are firm, not soft or limp. Your sense of smell can help you too. Melons and pineapples are ripe when you can smell their sweet scent.

Refrigerated Foods

Foods spoil in your fridge if you leave them there too long. And who knows how much time they spent at the grocery store before you bought them? But you can make sure what you buy is fresh by looking at the date on the package. Meat, poultry, and fish are all marked with "use by" dates. Dairy foods and egg cartons are marked with dates too. After this date you can't be sure the food is safe to eat.

Packaged Foods

Almost anything in a box, bag, can, or carton has a nutrition label that tells you the amount of fat, sugar, protein, carbohydrates, and calories in the food. Check this out before you buy. The "best if used by" date on the package gives you a sense of how long the food has been sitting on the shelf. Go for packages with dates that are well after the date you are shopping.

Organics

Many grocery stores sell organic foods. Organic fruits and vegetables are grown without harmful pesticides and other artificial chemicals that could be a danger to both you and the environment. Organic meats come from animals that are raised in a more natural environment and have not been given antibiotics or hormones.

Down on The Farm

The best way to shop for fresh food? Towns and cities often hold farmers markets where local farmers sell their products. You can also visit pick-your-own farms. Even better, you can grow your own garden in your backyard, on your apartment building's rooftop (if it's allowed), or in a community garden plot.

... Upsetting The Grownups.

Some adults can't handle a mess. You can always close the door to your bedroom or kick something under the couch in the family room. But you can't hide a mess in the kitchen.

Clean up your mess as you cook so there is less to deal with at the end. Toss the spoon in the sink or dishwasher when you're done stirring the pancake batter. Put the milk right back in the fridge. Throw out banana peels and mop up spills so you don't slip. And when you're all done, wash the dishes and the counters and wipe off the stovetop (once it's cool, of course).

If a parent, guardian, or other adult stands over your shoulder and tries to help, say you're the chef for the morning. But if you do need help—especially with something you've never done before—just ask. They'll appreciate the attention, and you'll both appreciate a day that doesn't begin with the kitchen blowing up.

... Burning The House Down.

Just a little flame can light a whole house on fire. And if you have a gas stove, you already have that little flame. You don't want it any bigger.

Be aware of what you wear. Long, loose sleeves or an untied apron can easily ignite. So can towels and oven mitts. Make sure to push up your sleeves, tie your apron, and never place something flammable close to a burner. Keep a fire extinguisher in the kitchen.

... A Trip To The Emergency Room.

Knives are sharp, and that's good. A sharp knife is actually safer than a dull one. If you're cutting a piece of fruit, a dull knife is more likely to slip off the surface and cut your finger. A sharp knife will cut right through your fruit. But you need to watch while you work. Use a cutting board, and always cut away from you.

Turn pot handles in, not out over the edge of the stove, where you can bump them and tip the pots over. Open the lid of a pot away from you so you don't get a face full of hot steam. Protect yourself with oven mitts when taking things out of the oven or holding the handle or top of a metal pot. And never pour water into a pan with hot oil—it will pop and splatter.

If you use a plug-in appliance, be sure the cord's not stretched across an area where someone could trip. Don't turn on an appliance if your hand is wet or use it too near the sink or a puddle of water. And don't reach into a blender or toaster or any appliance that's plugged in.

... Seeing Your Breakfast Come Back Again.

Using spoiled, expired, or unclean food can make you sick. A steaming spoonful of oatmeal might look great on the spoon. It doesn't look that good coming back again.

So how can you make sure your food stays down, where it's supposed to be? You need to get rid of bacteria. Before you cook, wash your hands with hot water and soap (not just a quick pass under a cold trickle). Gently rub fruits and vegetables under cool running water. High temperatures kill bacteria, so cook meat and eggs completely. Low temperatures slow the growth of bacteria, so keep all meats, eggs, dairy products, and most fruits and vegetables in the fridge. If something smells or looks funny or feels mushy, don't eat it.

Wash cutting boards and knives well. The hot water of the dishwasher kills bacteria best. Keep countertops, towels, and kitchen gear clean too. Trust me—you do not want to see what happens to an unwashed fork after a few days in a dark drawer.

HOW TO USE THIS BOOK

Each recipe has a list of ingredients called Food Stuff and a list of cooking tools called Kitchen Gear. Next comes the Prep Steps—instructions for whipping up a quick, healthy breakfast.

Don't panic—you may have to do some math. If you want to make more than the serving size mentioned in a recipe, you can double the ingredients. If you want to make less, cut them in half.

If you come across a cooking technique that you don't know (what does beat, fry, or knead mean anyway?!), flip back to the Technique Glossary (page 58).

Look to the Tools Glossary (page 56) to learn the difference between a spoon and a spatula and all the other kitchen gear.

Conversion Charts

WEIGHT

UNITED STATES	METRIC
1 ounce	30 grams
½ pound	225 g
1 pound	455 g

TEMPERATURE

DEGREES FAHRENHEIT	DEGREES CELSIUS
250°F	120°C
300°F	150°C
350°F	180°C
375°F	190°C
400°F	200°C
425°F	220°C

Look for special stamps on some recipes:

Most of these recipes can be made in the morning in just minutes. But some take longer. Look for the *Night Before* stamp on recipes that take more preparation. You can make them when you have more time. Then they'll be ready for a breakfast on the go.

Check out the *If You're a Vegetarian* stamp. Here you'll find foods to replace the nonvegetarian items in the Food Stuff lists.

Even if you're not a vegetarian, you still may want to change a recipe. Look for the *Call in the Subs* stamp to find out about alternative ingredients.

TURN OFF THE ALARM AND GET YOURSELF TO THE KITCHEN. SEIZE THE DAY, STARTING WITH A GOOD BREAKFAST.

VOLUME	UNITED STATES	METRIC
	¼ teaspoon	1 milliliter
	½ teaspoon	2.5 mL
	1 teaspoon	5 mL
	1 tablespoon	15 mL
	¼ cup	60 mL
	⅓ cup	80 mL
	½ cup	120 mL
	1 cup	250 mL
	1 quart	1 liter

YOU CAN'T BEAT EGGS!

Actually, you *can* beat eggs.

You can also fry them, boil them, and bake them. Eggs are so versatile that you can easily cook one for yourself—or a dozen for a crowd—without a lot of work.

— — — — — —

Brunch (that's a combination of breakfast and lunch) can be the central meal of a party. Invite the team back to your place after an early morning football game. Cook up a huge batch of eggs to match their massive appetites.

Or how about brinner? (That's breakfast and dinner). There's no rule that says you can't have omelets after 5 p.m. Friends and families bond over brinner!

SKYSCRAPER SANDWICH

Construction workers weld, haul, and hammer a thousand feet up to build the world's tallest skyscrapers. Why not build a tower of flavor right on the kitchen table? If you have a big appetite in the morning, try a breakfast sandwich. Between your bread basement and roof, you can add as many "floors" as you want. Your sandwich will tower over all the other breakfasts on the table.

Food Stuff

1 crusty roll
Vegetable cooking spray
1 large egg
Cheddar cheese, one slice
Avocado
Tomato
Lean deli ham, one slice

Kitchen Gear

Toaster
Plate
Medium skillet
Turner
Knife

Makes one sandwich

Prep Steps

1. Slice the crusty roll in half. Toast both halves in the toaster and set aside on the plate.

2. With a sharp knife, slice the avocado and tomato. Set aside.

3. Spray the skillet with cooking spray. Heat the skillet on medium to medium high. Crack the egg and pour its contents into the skillet.

4. Fry the egg for about 1½ minutes on one side. Flip the egg with a turner, and cook for another minute or until the white is completely solid and the yolk is close to completely solid.

5. Place the slice of cheese on top of the egg and cook until it just melts. With your turner, transfer the cheesy egg from the skillet to the bottom half of the roll.

6. Stack the ham and several slices of the avocado and tomato onto your egg.

7. Top your sandwich with the top half of the roll. Take a bite!

Spray Oil vs. Butter

Vegetable cooking spray is vegetable oil in an aerosol container. It keeps food from sticking to pans when you cook. You can also use butter or margarine. But spray oil helps you use less fat. If you would rather use butter, use a small amount—just enough to coat the bottom of the pan.

How To Crack an Egg

To crack an egg, hold it in your palm with your index finger on the narrow tip. Tap it firmly on the counter or the edge of an empty cup or bowl (not the bowl holding your mixture, in case some shell pieces fall in). Place both thumbs at the edges of the crack and pull the shell apart over the empty bowl. The white and yolk will fall into the bowl. Discard the shells. Then add the egg to your skillet or mixture.

If You're a Vegetarian

Don't use ham. Instead add more vegetables. Spinach and peppers (raw or cooked) are just two of the many vegetables that taste great in a sandwich.

SCRAMBLED SALSA BURRITO

It's not easy to eat scrambled eggs with your hands. You probably don't want to try, unless the eggs are wrapped in a neat package. This burrito is easy to pick up and even easier to eat.

Food Stuff

Vegetable cooking spray

2 large eggs

1 whole wheat tortilla

¼ cup Monterey jack cheese, shredded

¼ cup black beans, drained and rinsed

¼ cup fresh salsa

Makes one burrito

Kitchen Gear

Medium skillet

Bowl

Whisk

Wooden spoon

Plate

Dry measuring cups

Spoon

Prep Steps

1. Spray the skillet with cooking spray. Heat the skillet on medium to medium high.

2. Crack the eggs into a bowl. Beat together with a whisk.

3. Pour the eggs into the skillet. Using a wooden spoon, constantly scrape the skillet to scramble the eggs for about 1 to 1½ minutes until all eggs are dry with no wet spots. Set aside.

Yellow Yolks

The color of the yolk depends on what the hen eats. Marigold petals, which are bright yellow and orange, are sometimes added to hens' feed to make yolks brighter.

4. Lay the tortilla on a plate. Place the eggs in the center of the tortilla. Sprinkle with the cheese and black beans. Spoon on the salsa.

5. Fold the tortilla to hold in your ingredients (see opposite page). Pick it up and eat!

How To Fold a Burrito

You don't want your eggs spilling out onto the plate. Lay the tortilla flat. Place the eggs in the center, fairly close to the top, and leave some room on the bottom. Fold the bottom edge over the eggs. Then close the other two sides, like a jacket. The eggs will poke out the top.

QUICK QUICHES

Quick quiz! How many food groups can you fit in one bite? All of them! A quiche has dairy products, meat, veggies, and bread in one dish.

Food Stuff

2 large eggs
½ cup milk
2 strips bacon
4 to 6 cherry tomatoes
3 to 6 slices whole grain bread
Vegetable cooking spray
½ cup cheddar cheese, shredded

Kitchen Gear

Mixing bowl
Liquid measuring cup
Dry measuring cups
Whisk
3-inch (7.6-centimeter) round cookie cutter or drinking glass
Muffin pan
Knife

Makes six muffin-sized quiches

Prep Steps

1. Preheat the oven to 400°F.

2. Crack the eggs into a bowl. Add the milk. Beat with a whisk. Set aside.

3. Cook the bacon in the microwave until crispy (see opposite page). Crush it into small pieces. Set aside.

4. Cut the tomatoes into thin slices. Set aside.

5. With a 3-inch (7.6-cm) round cookie cutter, or the mouth of a 3-inch-wide glass, cut six circles from the bread. Depending on the size of the bread, you may be able to get one or two circles from each slice. (Keep the scraps of bread to use as breadcrumbs in another recipe, or feed them to the birds.)

6. Spray six of the cups in the muffin pan with cooking spray. Place a bread circle in each muffin cup. Press it into the bottom and up the sides of the cup.

7. Sprinkle the cheese and crumbled bacon into each of the bread cups. Pour the egg mixture on top, distributing it evenly among the cups. Lay about three slices of tomatoes on top of each one.

8. Bake at 400°F for 10 minutes. Turn down the oven temperature to 350°F. Bake for another 10 minutes or until a toothpick inserted in the center of a quiche comes out clean.

9. Run a knife around the edges of the muffin cups to loosen the quiches and take them out of the muffin pan.

The Toothpick Test

To see whether baked goods are done, chefs often use the toothpick test. When you think your food has finished baking, insert a toothpick in the center and pull it out again. If there is gooey batter or egg clinging to the toothpick, the food needs to bake longer. But if the toothpick comes out relatively clean, you can turn off the oven and enjoy your creation!

Cooking Bacon in The Microwave

Cooking bacon in the microwave on a plate with paper towels prevents bacon fat from spurting out of an open skillet, and the towels soak up some of the fat.

1. Lay two pieces of paper towel on a microwave-safe plate. Lay your pieces of bacon on the paper towels. Place another paper towel on top.

2. Microwave on high for 3 minutes. Check on the bacon. Add another minute as needed. Keep checking and adding minutes until the bacon is crispy.

If You're a Vegetarian

You can omit the bacon. If you still want that bacon flavor, look for soy bacon in the vegetarian section of your grocery store.

HIDDEN SUNSHINE FRENCH TOAST

Allez, debout les feinéants! That's French for "wake up, lazy bones!"
(It's pronounced *ALLay, day-boo lay fay nawnts,* in case you want to
try it on your parents when they're sleeping in.) The weatherperson
might report a gray and dreary day. Maybe you have to get up while
it's still dark outside. That's OK—it's French toast to the rescue!
Peek between these two slices of bread to find a sunny surprise.

Food Stuff

1 large egg

3 tablespoons milk

1 tablespoon maple syrup

¼ teaspoon cinnamon

¼ teaspoon vanilla

2 slices whole grain bread

Vegetable cooking spray

1 slice canned pineapple ring

Maple syrup or cinnamon sugar for topping

Kitchen Gear

Shallow bowl

Measuring spoons

Whisk

Large skillet

Turner

Plate

Makes one serving

Prep Steps

1. Break the egg into a shallow bowl and beat
   with a whisk so that the yolk and white are well
   combined. Beat in the milk, syrup, cinnamon,
   and vanilla.

2. Soak each slice of bread in the egg mixture.

3. Spray the skillet with cooking spray. Heat on
   medium high.

4. Lay the two slices of bread in the pan. Cook for
   2 minutes. Flip them over with a turner. Cook
   for another minute or until lightly browned.

5. On a plate, layer one slice of bread, the ring of
   pineapple, and the other slice of bread. Top with
   syrup or sprinkle with cinnamon sugar.

PARTY CAKES

Layers of pancakes topped with sweet "frosting" and sprinkles look just like a birthday cake. So what if it's not your birthday? Add a candle and start your day with a party.

Food Stuff

½ cup old-fashioned oats

½ cup whole wheat flour

2 teaspoons sugar

1 teaspoon baking soda

¼ teaspoon salt

1 large egg, lightly beaten

½ teaspoon vanilla

½ cup + 2 tablespoons milk

1 tablespoon rainbow sprinkles

Vegetable cooking spray

1 6-ounce container nonfat vanilla yogurt

1 tablespoon maple syrup

Kitchen Gear

Large mixing bowl

Dry measuring cups

Liquid measuring cup

Measuring spoons

Whisk

Large skillet

Bowl

Plate

Makes eight 4-inch (10-cm) pancakes

Prep Steps

1. In a large bowl, mix the oats, flour, sugar, baking soda, salt, egg, vanilla, and milk with a whisk.

2. Spray the skillet with cooking spray. Heat on medium to medium high.

3. With a small measuring cup, scoop the batter onto the skillet. Cook the pancake for about 2 to 2½ minutes or until bubbles form on the top. Flip the pancake with your turner to the other side. Cook about 2 minutes more or until the bottom is browned. Set aside.

4. Continue scooping the batter and cooking the pancakes until all the batter is used up.

Tips for Measuring Flour

Flour needs to be light and airy to get an accurate measurement. If you need a cup of flour, don't dip the whole one-cup measuring cup into your flour bag and pull it out. The flour will be too tightly packed inside. Instead, spoon the flour into the cup a little at a time. Level off the top with the straight side of a table knife so it is completely flat and level with the brim. Then you'll have the right amount.

5. To make the "frosting" for your pancakes, empty the yogurt into a bowl. Stir in the maple syrup.

6. To serve your pancakes, place one on a plate. Spread it with the yogurt mixture. Layer on another pancake and spread with yogurt. Add a few sprinkles for decoration.

Call in the Subs

Try different flavored yogurts for the icing. (You might not want to mix in the maple syrup, though. Blueberry-maple syrup isn't to everyone's taste.)

BREAKFAST BOWLS

BowL. Spoon. EaT.
'Nuf said.

25

OATMEAL CHOCOLATE CHIP COOKIE IN A BOWL

Cookies and milk for breakfast? Here's a way to have a morning treat and still please your parents. Oatmeal is a good-for-you whole grain. Add the same ingredients that go into an oatmeal chocolate chip cookie, and you have a sweet breakfast.

Food Stuff

½ cup instant oats

½ cup milk

1 teaspoon brown sugar

1 tablespoon chocolate chips

1 tablespoon chopped walnuts

Kitchen Gear

Microwave-safe bowl

Liquid measuring cup

Dry measuring cups

Spoon

Microwave

Measuring spoons

Makes one serving

Prep Steps

1. In a microwave-safe bowl, stir together the oats and milk.

2. Microwave uncovered on high for 1½ minutes. Stir with a spoon. Microwave for another 30 seconds if the oatmeal isn't warm enough. Take out of the microwave and let it sit for a moment.

Give a Cow a Break!

If you want to try some other types of milk instead of cow's milk, you have some choices. Soy milk is widely available in grocery stores. Milk is also made from rice, oats, and even nuts, such as almonds.

3. Add the brown sugar, chocolate chips, and walnuts to the oatmeal. Stir them in.

4. If the oatmeal is too hot, or you want it to be less lumpy, add a splash of milk.

Call in the Subs

If you want your oatmeal to taste like an oatmeal raisin cookie, replace the chocolate chips with 1 tablespoon of raisins.

POWER CEREAL

A monster truck rally roars with excitement. Mauled cars and metal debris are strewn about the arena. Will the next opponent have the power to crush the competition? Suddenly something emerges from the clouds of dust ...

It's a bowl of cereal! And it's packed with so much healthy power you won't know what hit you.

Food Stuff

1 cup crisp oat cereal squares
1 tablespoon wheat germ
2 tablespoons slivered almonds
2 tablespoons dried cranberries

Kitchen Gear

Dry measuring cups
Measuring spoons
Bowl

Makes one serving

Prep Steps

1. Combine all of the ingredients in a bowl.
2. Pour in milk, and enjoy!

Call in the Subs

Any healthy whole grain cereal without added sugar will work for this recipe. So will any variety of nuts and dried fruit. If you have a bunch of cereals that are getting low and aren't enough for a serving, mix them together to create a multigrain cereal bowl!

BANANA CREAM PIE IN A BOWL

Pie-eating champions don't eat their pie in neat triangles. They eat it by smashing their faces right into the pan. Who cares if they get nostrils full of pie? Until you're a champion, how about eating pie from a bowl with a spoon instead?

Food Stuff

1 6-ounce container nonfat vanilla yogurt

1 ripe banana

¼ cup granola

¼ cup graham cracker crumbs (about 1 graham cracker)

Kitchen Gear

Bowl

Knife

Dry measuring cups

Spoon

Makes one serving

Prep Steps

1. Empty the container of yogurt into a bowl.

2. Slice the banana into small pieces and add to the yogurt.

3. Add the granola and graham cracker crumbs.

4. Stir gently to combine ingredients. Dig in!

Crushing Graham Crackers

Why did the graham cracker go to the doctor? Because he felt crummy!

To make graham cracker crumbs, place the cracker in a sealed plastic bag. Lay it on the counter. Smash the bag with your open hand until the cracker has broken into tiny pieces. You can also roll over the bag with a rolling pin, or bang it with the bottom of a measuring cup.

ON THE GO

IT's not your fault that you rush in the morning!

The alarm didn't go off, your sister hogged the bathroom, and the dog hid your shoes. You certainly don't have time for a sit-down breakfast!

Here are some portable breakfasts to carry with you on the way to school.

SMOOTH MOVES

Are you slower than a snail? Moving like molasses? Going at a glacial pace? Get it in gear and make this quick breakfast in a glass. Toss in some ingredients, press a button, and you have yourself a smoothie.

Food Stuff

¾ cup milk

1 6-ounce container flavored yogurt

1 cup of fresh or frozen fruit

Extras (see chart below)

Kitchen Gear

Liquid measuring cup

Dry measuring cups

Blender

Spoon

Knife

Glass or travel mug

CHILL OUT!

Frozen fruit works well for a smoothie. It takes less time to prepare and adds a frosty bite to your drink.

Prep Steps

1. Pour the milk into the blender.

2. Spoon in the yogurt.

3. If you use fresh fruit, cut it into small chunks and be sure to take out any pits or seeds.

4. Add the fruit and any extras to the blender.

5. Put the top on the blender. Blend for about 30 seconds. Pour it into a glass or travel mug.

Makes one serving

Call in the Subs

The good thing about smoothies is that you can experiment with flavor combinations. Here's a mix and match chart for smoothie ideas. Choose a yogurt, fruit, and extra, mix them, and slurp it up!

YOGURT	FRUIT	EXTRAS
vanilla	raspberries	1 tablespoon wheat germ
berry flavors	pineapple	splash of coconut milk
black cherry	cherries	1 tablespoon peanut butter
pineapple	bananas	1 tablespoon maple syrup
lemon	peaches	1 tablespoon honey
chocolate	blueberries	sprinkle of cinnamon
lime	mangoes	

TRY THESE COMBINATIONS:

Vanilla + pineapple + coconut milk = Tropical Paradise

Chocolate + banana + peanut butter = Peanut Butter Cup

Lemon + peaches + honey = Summer Surprise

Berry flavor + blueberries + maple syrup + cinnamon + wheat germ = Blueberry Cobbler

Blend by Hand?

Instead of a regular blender, you can use a hand blender. This blender in wand form makes smoothie preparation a breeze, and it takes up less kitchen space than a regular blender.

GO NUTS NUGGETS

In 1849 eager prospectors hurried west in search of nuggets of precious gold. They had a hard life, and very few struck it rich. You'll have more luck than they did finding golden nuggets—right in your own kitchen.

Food Stuff

1½ cups toasted oat cereal

1½ cups puffed wheat cereal

¼ cup dried fruit, such as raisins, cranberries, cherries, or blueberries

¼ cup walnuts

¼ cup pecans

¼ cup peanuts

3 tablespoons sunflower seeds

1 tablespoon butter

2 cups mini marshmallows

Vegetable cooking spray

Kitchen Gear

Dry measuring cups

Measuring spoons

Large bowl

2-quart saucepan

Spoon

Spatula

8 x 8-inch (20 x 20-cm) baking pan

Wax paper

Knife

Makes about 16 squares

Prep Steps

1. In a large bowl, mix the cereals, dried fruit, walnuts, pecans, peanuts, and sunflower seeds.

2. In a saucepan, melt the butter over medium low heat. Add the marshmallows. Stir with a spoon, scraping the sides, until the marshmallows melt. Keep a close eye to be sure the marshmallows don't burn. It only takes a few minutes.

3. Take the saucepan off the heat. Pour the melted marshmallows into the bowl over the cereal mixture. Stir with a spatula so that the marshmallow is evenly distributed. Be sure to mix in the heavier bits (nuts and fruit) that may sink to the bottom of the bowl.

4. Spray an 8 x 8-inch (20 x 20-cm) square baking pan with cooking spray. Pour the mixture into the pan.

5. Spray a piece of wax paper with cooking spray. Press it over the top of the mixture to flatten it.

6. Place the pan covered with the wax paper in the refrigerator to cool for about half an hour. Cut into squares.

Night Before

Make these on the weekend, and store them in an airtight container in the fridge or at room temperature. They will last for a few days—unless you eat them all the day you make them!

BAD BREATH BAGELS

Do you like to spread out on your bus seat? Especially if you have a backpack, sports gear, or a musical instrument, you may not want to cram in another person too. If someone tries to sit down, just say "hi!" after eating one of these bagels. The person will find another seat, and you'll have lots of room for yourself.*

Food Stuff

4 ounces light cream cheese, room temperature

½ teaspoon parsley

⅛ teaspoon garlic powder

⅛ teaspoon black pepper

⅛ teaspoon thyme

⅛ teaspoon marjoram

⅛ teaspoon dill

1 whole grain bagel

Kitchen Gear

Bowl

Measuring spoons

Spoon for stirring

Toaster

Knife for spreading

Makes one serving

Prep Steps

1. In a small bowl, blend the cream cheese, parsley, garlic powder, black pepper, thyme, marjoram, and dill with a spoon.

2. Toast the bagel in the toaster.

3. Spread the cream cheese on the bagel. Wrap it in a napkin and you're ready to go!

Spice Raid!

It's fun to raid the spice cabinet. Try various combinations of spices to find another winning (and aromatic) seasoning mix.

*If you actually want to keep your friends, you may want to pop a breath mint after you eat your bagel. Or simply omit the garlic powder from the recipe. Garlic is tasty, but the flavor does hang on your breath for a while!

Night Before

You can make this spread the night before so you don't have to mix it in the morning. You can just spread it on your bagel and go. It also serves as a tasty dip for veggies or a spread for crackers or sandwiches.

You need to eat breakfast, but your phone's ringing. There's not time to eat *and* hear about the drama on your BFF's swim team. What to do? Do both! You can hold the phone—and a scone—at the same time. If only you could talk and chew at the same time ...

Food Stuff

1½ cups whole wheat flour

½ cup cornmeal

1½ teaspoons baking powder

½ teaspoon baking soda

¼ teaspoon salt

½ cup chopped pecans

½ cup raisins

⅓ cup maple syrup

¾ cup canned pumpkin

1 large egg, lightly beaten

¼ teaspoon vanilla

Vegetable cooking spray

¼ cup orange juice

Cinnamon sugar

Makes 16 small scones

Kitchen Gear

Liquid measuring cup

Dry measuring cups

Measuring spoons

Large bowl

Medium bowl

Spatula

Knife

Baking sheet

Pastry brush

Prep Steps

1. Preheat the oven to 400° F.

2. In a large bowl, mix the flour, cornmeal, baking powder, baking soda, salt, pecans, and raisins. In medium bowl, mix the maple syrup, pumpkin, egg, and vanilla.

3. Add the wet mixture to the flour mixture. Stir with a spatula until the mixtures combine to form a dough.

4. Sprinkle some flour on a flat surface. Take out half of the dough. Knead the dough about five times. Then roll it into a ball.

5. Flatten the dough into a 1-inch (2.5-cm) thick circle. Cut the circle into eight equal triangle pieces. Repeat steps 4 and 5 with the other half of the dough.

6. Spray a baking sheet with cooking spray. Place the scones a few inches apart. With a pastry brush, coat each scone with the orange juice. Sprinkle cinnamon sugar on each one.

7. Bake at 400° F for eight to 10 minutes, or until a toothpick inserted in the center of a scone comes out clean.

Night Before

Baking takes time, so take time to bake. Grabbing an already-made scone in the morning takes only a few seconds of your day!

PB&J MUFFINS

The boxers are ready. In one corner of the ring: grape. In the other: raspberry. And wait—strawberry and peach are itching to join the fight. They all want to get beaten into a delicious muffin! But there's no need to put on the boxing gloves. All jellies will work for this recipe.

Food Stuff

½ cup old-fashioned oats

1¾ cups whole wheat flour

2 teaspoons baking powder

½ cup peanut butter

¼ cup honey

¼ cup applesauce

¾ cup milk

1 egg, lightly beaten

Jam or jelly, any flavor

Vegetable cooking spray

Kitchen Gear

Large bowl

Dry measuring cups

Liquid measuring cup

Measuring spoons

Spatula

Muffin pan

Spoon

Knife

Makes 12 muffins

Prep Steps

1. Preheat the oven to 375° F.

2. In a large bowl, mix the oats, flour, and baking powder. Add the peanut butter and honey. Mix together with a spatula, or with your hand, until you have a crumbly dough.

3. Add the applesauce, milk, and egg. Mix until all of the ingredients are just combined. Do not overmix.

4. Spray the muffin pan with cooking spray. Spoon one heaping tablespoon of batter into the bottom of each muffin cup. Spoon 1 teaspoon of jelly on top of the batter. Cover the jelly with another spoonful of batter.

5. Bake at 375° F for 15 to 18 minutes, or until lightly browned and a toothpick inserted in the center comes out clean.

6. Let cool, and then remove the muffins from the pan by circling the edges gently with a knife.

Night Before

If you make the muffins ahead of time, you can just grab one and go in the morning—and the next 11 mornings as well. (Or five if you eat two at a time!)

Call in the Subs

If you're allergic to peanut butter, you may be able to use other "butters" made from nuts. You can buy almond butter, cashew butter, and sunflower seed butter. But check with a parent or other adult before you try any substitutions in case peanuts aren't your only allergy. And always check labels carefully to be sure a product is completely peanut-free.

ON THE SIDE

A hero is never as brave, strong, or dashing without a sidekick.

Batman has Robin.
Holmes has Watson.
Ketchup has mustard.

Some breakfasts need a sidekick too.

Fruits and drinks help complete a meal.

MOHAWK MANGO HEADS

Who's that dude with the Mohawk haircut? It's not a new kid in the neighborhood. It's a mango! He's sweet. He's spiky. He's downright delicious. How can something so cool be so good for you?

Mango Man. Even your parents will approve.

Food Stuff

1 ripe mango

Kitchen Gear

Knife

Prep Steps

Makes two mango heads

1. Place the mango on its tip. Cut off one of the sides as close to the pit as you can. You'll have a "bowl" shaped slice of mango.

2. Cut five lines into the flesh of the mango from top to bottom. Don't cut too deep. You don't want to cut through the skin.

3. Cut five lines the opposite way to make a grid.

4. Push up on the skin side of your mango "bowl." The grid of lines will open up, and the skin will hold your pieces together.

5. Repeat on the other side of the mango to make another mango head.

Give Your Mango Head a Haircut

You can eat the mango right off the skin this way. It's like giving him a haircut! And don't waste the extra mango still attached to the pit. Cut as much mango flesh off the pit as you can. Slice it and eat it with a fork.

He's Hot!

Try sprinkling your mango head with chili powder to spice him up!

APES AND GRAPES SALAD

If you are a scout, you probably know the song "I Like Bananas, Coconuts, and Grapes." If not, try this breakfast treat and get a taste of what everyone is singing about!

Food Stuff

½ cup white or red seedless grapes (15 to 20 small grapes)

½ of one banana

2 tablespoons flaked coconut

Makes one serving

Kitchen Gear

Dry measuring cups

Measuring spoons

Colander

Knife

Bowl

Spoon

Prep Steps

1. Rinse and drain the grapes in the colander. Cut the grapes in half. Place them in a bowl.

2. Peel the banana and cut it into small pieces. Add it to the bowl.

3. Sprinkle the coconut on top. Mix gently with a spoon.

Call in the Subs

Tarzan of the Apes liked other fruits too. You can make this fruit salad with pretty much any fruit. If you want to stick to tropical fruits, try pineapple, mango, papaya, or guava.

48

ORANGE CREAM JUICE

There's no wooden stick in this juicy, creamy, icy treat. And no drippy melting mess. Just foamy goodness to suck up with a straw.

Food Stuff

¾ cup soy milk

3 tablespoons orange juice concentrate

Makes one serving

Kitchen Gear

Liquid measuring cup

Measuring spoons

Blender

Glass

Straw

Prep Steps

1. Pour the milk into the blender.

2. Add the orange juice concentrate.

3. Put the top on the blender. Blend for about 30 seconds. Pour the juice into a glass. Drink with a straw.

Call in the Subs

Soy milk gives this drink a nice creamy texture, but you can use regular milk too. If you make it with grape juice concentrate instead of orange juice concentrate, it's called a purple cow.

RED-HOT COCOA

Fire alarm! Luckily the kitchen's not on fire. It's your mouth! Wake up instantly with a kick of chili powder and cinnamon hidden in with the chocolate. It's HOT hot cocoa that will really spice up your morning.

Food Stuff

1½ cups milk

2½ tablespoons unsweetened cocoa powder

2 tablespoons sugar

½ teaspoon cinnamon

⅛ teaspoon chili powder

¼ teaspoon vanilla

Kitchen Gear

Glass measuring cup

Spoon

Large mug

Measuring spoons

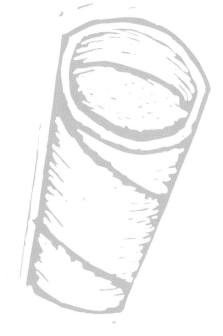

Makes one serving

Prep Steps

1. In the microwave, heat the milk in a microwave-safe glass measuring cup on high for 1 minute. Stir. Heat for another 30 seconds to 1 minute until hot. Set aside.

2. In the mug, add the cocoa powder, sugar, cinnamon, and chili powder. Mix all of these dry ingredients together with a spoon.

3. Add the vanilla to the mug. Then pour in a few tablespoons of the hot milk. Stir until no more lumps of dry ingredients remain.

4. Pour in the rest of the milk gradually, stirring all the time.

Night Before

Increase the dry ingredient amounts (cocoa powder, sugar, cinnamon, and chili powder) and store the mixture in an airtight container. In the morning, you just need to measure out 4 tablespoons (less or more if you like it weaker or stronger) into a mug, add the vanilla, warm milk, and enjoy!

CHEW ON THIS!

After a long trip, the family car might be running low on gas. Your body is your vehicle. While you sleep, your body uses up a lot of its fuel too. This means that when you wake up in the morning, you're running on empty. Just as the driver refills the car's gas tank, you have to refuel your body. If you don't fill it up in the morning, you may feel tired and have trouble concentrating.

To feel your best, you need good fuel. It's important to learn about the kinds of fuel you're eating.

CARBOHYDRATES

Carbohydrates are sugar. That's right—sugar. Your body turns carbohydrates into energy. So if you think your body craves sugar, you're right. But not all carbohydrates are created equal. You can find good carbs in grains, fruits, and vegetables.

Grains: Wheat, rice, oats, and corn are all grains. They are used to make items such as cereal, bread, waffles, pancakes, oatmeal, and muffins. Whole grains are best. They're chock-full of nutrients and also contain fiber, which helps keep food moving through your digestive system. Avoid refined grains, like the kind used to make white bread. Most of the nutrients have been removed to make them "white."

Fruits and vegetables: Fruits and veggies have vitamins and minerals your body needs. You can choose everything from tiny blueberries to huge honeydew melons. Vegetables are great for breakfast too—tomatoes, onions, peppers, and spinach are especially tasty in egg dishes.

PROTEIN

Protein builds your bones, muscles, and body tissues. You can find it in these breakfast foods:

Meat and beans: Bacon, sausage, and ham all have protein. So do black beans, soybeans, and many others. If you choose meat, look for lean cuts. And you can find more healthy versions of bacon and sausage made from turkey or soy.

Eggs: Buy them by the dozen, and then try to find a dozen ways to cook them.

Nuts: Peanuts, almonds, cashews, walnuts, pistachios, and other nuts pack a big protein punch in a small package.

Dairy products: Not only do foods made from milk have protein, but they're also high in calcium, which helps build bones. Seek out low-fat or nonfat versions of milk, ice cream, cheese, and yogurt.

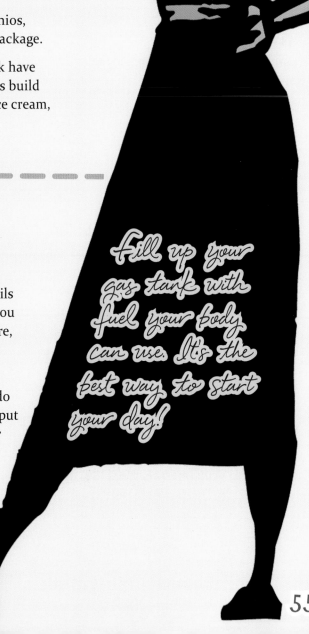

Fill up your gas tank with fuel your body can use. It's the best way to start your day!

FAT

Yes, fat! The fat in your body stores your energy. So you do need it ... but not too much. The fat found in nuts, some vegetables (such as avocados), and plant oils (such as vegetable oil or sunflower oil) are better for you than solid fats. Solid fats are solid at room temperature, like the kind found in butter, cheese, and bacon.

You'll probably never need to add fat to your diet, because so many foods already have fat in them. But do try to reduce sources of fat. In fact, you don't need to put any butter on that toast when there are so many other spreads to choose from!

You may have noticed that some recipes in this book use fat and sugar. Relax! If most of the foods you choose to eat are packed with nutrients, then it's OK to treat yourself once in a while.

Fill up your gas tank with fuel your body can use. It's the best way to start your day.

TOOLS GLOSSARY

Baking pan
flat metal pan with high sides for baking cakes and brownies

Baking sheet
flat metal pan used to bake cookies and other baked goods

Blender
appliance with a rotating blade that mixes solids and liquids

Colander
bowl dotted with holes to drain liquids from foods

Dry measuring cups
containers the size of specific standard measurements. Dry cups come in ¼ cup, ⅓ cup, ½ cup, and 1 cup sizes. Measure dry ingredients over an empty bowl, not over your mixture, in case of spills. Level off dry ingredients with a table knife.

Liquid measuring cup
container marked at intervals along the sides to accurately measure amounts of liquid. A liquid measuring cup is usually marked at ¼ cup, ⅓ cup , ½ cup, ⅔ cup, ¾ cup, and 1 cup intervals. Hold the cup at eye level to check the measurement.

Measuring spoons
spoons the size of specific standard measurements. Measuring spoons come in ¼ teaspoon ½ teaspoon, 1 teaspoon, and 1 tablespoon measurements. There are 3 teaspoons in a tablespoon.

Microwave
appliance that cooks food with radio waves. Make sure the cup, bowl, or plate you use is microwave-safe. Microwaving heats food and the container it's in, so use oven mitts to remove it from the microwave.

Muffin pan
metal pan with six or 12 cups designed for baking muffins

Pastry brush
small brush used to apply liquids on top of foods

Saucepan
round, deep metal pan with a handle and a lid, used on a stovetop

Skillet
round, shallow metal pan with a handle, used on a stovetop

Spatula
flat tool used to mix ingredients or scrape the side of a bowl

Toaster
appliance that makes bread brown and crispy. Toasters load from the top. Toaster ovens have a door that opens in the front.

Turner
flat tool used to flip foods from one side to the other or to remove foods from a pan

Wax paper
paper coated with wax, used to cover foods

Whisk
tool made of looped metal wires used to add air into a mixture by beating it rapidly

TECHNIQUE GLOSSARY

Beat
stir very quickly to help add air to a mixture

Blend
mix together, often in a blender

Drain
remove liquid by pouring it off or placing it in a colander

Fry
cook something on a stovetop in hot fat

Knead
mix dough in a way to work the glutens (a type of protein found in flour). To knead dough, you flatten the dough with the heel of your hand, fold the dough in half, and press down again. Sprinkle your work surface with flour to keep the dough from sticking.

Melt
heat a food to turn it from solid to liquid

Preheat
turn the oven on ahead of time so it is at the correct temperature when you are ready to begin baking

Scramble
cook an egg mixture in a skillet. As the eggs cook, they turn from wet to dry. You need to constantly scrape the skillet and turn the cooked egg to the top and the liquid egg to the bottom so it cooks evenly.

Shred
cut into small thin strips, often with a grater

Slice
cut into thin pieces with a knife

Soak
completely cover in liquid

READ MORE

Carle, Megan, and Jill Carle. *Teens Cook: How to Cook What You Want to Eat.* Berkeley, Calif.: Ten Speed Press, 2004.

Dunnington, Rose. *Delicious Drinks to Sip, Slurp, Gulp & Guzzle.* New York: Lark Books, 2006.

Gold, Rozanne. *Eat Fresh Food: Awesome Recipes for Teen Chefs.* New York: Bloomsbury USA, 2009.

Schwartz, Ellen. *I'm a Vegetarian: Amazing Facts and Ideas for Healthy Vegetarians.* Plattsburgh, N.Y.: Tundra Books, 2002.

INTERNET SITES

Use FactHound to find Internet sites related to this book. All of the sites on FactHound have been researched by our staff.

Here's all you do:
Visit *www.facthound.com*
Type in this code: 9780756544072

ACKNOWLEDGEMENTS

Many thanks to friends and family members who sampled my creations and shared recipe advice. I am grateful to Paula Meachen, Patricia Rau, Denise Genest, and the Tuesday morning writers. Additional thanks to the teens of my neighborhood who e-mailed me lists of their favorite foods. An extra nod to Chris, Charlie, and Allison, who ate and drank the good and the bad and never held back their honest opinions.

Dana Meachen Rau

INDEX

allergy substitutions, 43
Apes and Grapes Salad, 48–49

bacon, microwaving, 19
bacteria, 9
Bad Breath Bagels, 38–39
Banana Cream Pie in a Bowl, 30–31
beans, 16, 55
burritos, folding, 17

carbohydrates, 7, 54
cleanup, 8, 9
cooking spray, 14

eggs, 15, 16, 55

farmers markets, 7
fats, 7, 14, 19, 55
fires, 8
flour, measuring, 22
freshness, 6, 7, 9
fruits, 6, 7, 9, 28, 34, 36, 46, 48, 54

Go Nuts Nuggets, 36–37
graham crackers, crushing, 30
grains, 26, 28, 54

hand blenders, 35
Hidden Sunshine French Toast, 20–21
Hold the Phone scones, 40–41

mangoes, eating, 46
meats, 6, 7, 9, 18, 55
milk, 8, 26, 50, 55
Mohawk Mango Heads, 46–47

"night before" preparation, 36, 39, 41, 42, 52
nutrition labels, 7
nuts, 26, 28, 36, 42, 43, 55

Oatmeal Chocolate Chip Cookie in a Bowl,
    26–27

Orange Cream Juice, 50–51
organic foods, 7

Party Cakes, 22–23
PB&J Muffins, 42–43
Power Cereal, 28–29
protein, 7, 55

Quick Quiches, 18–19

Red-Hot Cocoa, 52–53
refrigeration, 6

safety, 6, 8–9
Scrambled Salsa Burrito, 16–17
Skyscraper Sandwich, 14–15
Smooth Moves smoothie, 34–35
spices, 38, 47, 52
substitutions, 15, 19, 23, 27, 28, 34,
    43, 48, 50

toothpick test, 18

vegetables, 6, 9, 14, 18, 39, 54, 55
vegetarian substitutions, 15, 19

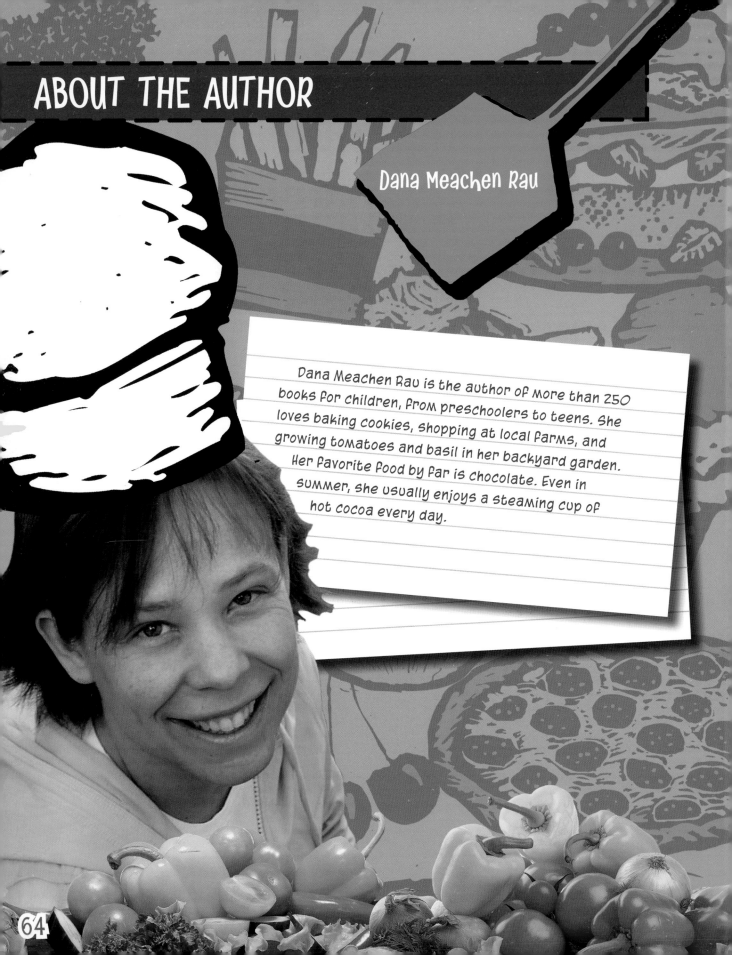

Dana Meachen Rau

Dana Meachen Rau is the author of more than 250 books for children, from preschoolers to teens. She loves baking cookies, shopping at local farms, and growing tomatoes and basil in her backyard garden. Her favorite food by far is chocolate. Even in summer, she usually enjoys a steaming cup of hot cocoa every day.